LET'S-READ-AND-FIND-OUT SCIENCE®

Falcons Nest on Skyscrapers

BY PRISCILLA BELZ JENKINS

ILLUSTRATED BY MEGAN LLOYD

HarperCollinsPublishers

With special thanks to Jean Craighead George, Dr. Tom Cade,
Dr. Charles Walcott, and USF&G Insurance.

The illustrations in this book were done with watercolor and pen and ink on Saunders Waterford Watercolor Paper.

The *Let's-Read-and-Find-Out Science* book series was originated by Dr. Franklyn M. Branley, Astronomer Emeritus and former Chairman of the American Museum–Hayden Planetarium, and was formerly co-edited by him and Dr. Roma Gans, Professor Emeritus of Childhood Education, Teachers College, Columbia University. Text and illustrations for each of the books in the series are checked for accuracy by an expert in the relevant field. For a complete catalog of Let's-Read-and-Find-Out Science books, write to HarperCollins Children's Books, 10 East 53rd Street, New York, NY 10022.

Library of Congress Cataloging-in-Publication Data
Jenkins, Priscilla Belz.
    Falcons nest on skyscrapers / by Priscilla Belz Jenkins ; illustrated by Megan Lloyd.
        p.   cm. — (Let's-read-and-find-out science. Stage 2)
    ISBN 0-06-021104-0. — ISBN 0-06-021105-9 (lib. bdg.)
    ISBN 0-06-445149-6 (pbk.)
    1. Peregrine falcon—Juvenile literature.   2. Peregrine falcon—Maryland—Baltimore—
Juvenile literature.   I. Lloyd, Megan, ill.   II. Title.   III. Series.
QL696.F34J46   1996   94-18701
598.9'18—dc20   CIP
                                                                             AC

Typography by Al Cetta
10 9 8 7 6 5 4 3 2 1
❖
First Edition

Falcons Nest
on Skyscrapers

Falcons are remarkable birds. They are the fastest, most skillful hunters on earth. Smart and sleek, beautiful and proud, falcons have been admired for thousands of years.

There are nearly forty different kinds of falcons, and they live in almost every part of the world. The gyrfalcon, the peregrine falcon, the merlin, the American kestrel, and the prairie falcon all live in the United States.

Hieroglyph for ancient
Egyptian falcon god, Horus.

Birds such as falcons, eagles, hawks, owls, and vultures are called birds of prey because they eat other birds and small animals. They help to keep pigeons, mice, and other small animals from becoming too plentiful.

No other creature can match a falcon's agility and remarkable powers of hearing and sight when it hunts. A falcon's body is designed for speed, and its aim is perfect.

When a falcon hunts, first it targets a moving victim, often a flying pigeon, one of its favorite foods. Then it circles high above its prey.

Suddenly the falcon aims and dives straight down at 200 miles per hour! This dive is called a stoop. After striking its prey, the falcon circles back, grabs the falling victim with hooklike talons, and carries it off to eat. The entire capture takes less than a minute.

Not long ago, peregrine falcons lived practically all over the world. But in the 1950s, they began to disappear very rapidly. No one knew why. Bird experts, or ornithologists, were alarmed. Something had to be done quickly, or the peregrines would become extinct.

Ornithologists began to solve the mystery by carefully watching falcons at their nests. They saw that when a mother peregrine sat on her eggs to keep them warm, they broke. Why would this happen?

After much searching, they found the answer: a poison known as DDT.

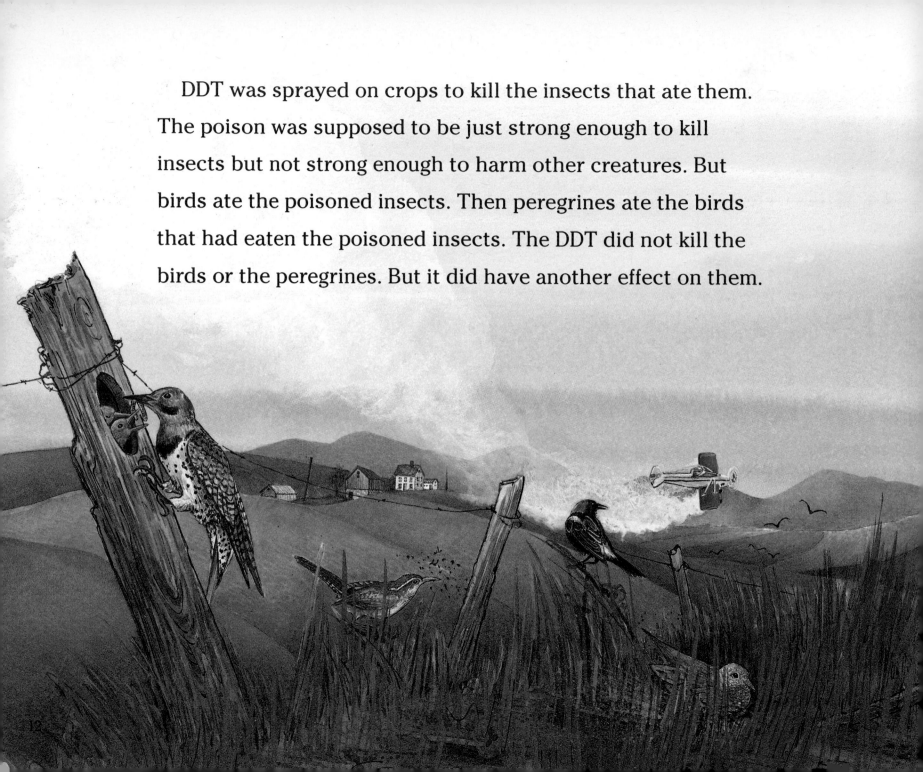

DDT was sprayed on crops to kill the insects that ate them. The poison was supposed to be just strong enough to kill insects but not strong enough to harm other creatures. But birds ate the poisoned insects. Then peregrines ate the birds that had eaten the poisoned insects. The DDT did not kill the birds or the peregrines. But it did have another effect on them.

The DDT made the peregrines' eggshells too thin. When the mother falcons sat on them, they broke. No baby falcons, or eyases, could hatch.

People in the United States stopped using DDT when they realized what it was doing to wildlife. But by then, the peregrine was nearing extinction.

Falcon researchers working at a special laboratory called The Hawk Barn were determined to save the peregrine falcon. They collected young peregrines from the wild and raised them in their lab. These birds mated and laid eggs. After the eggs hatched, the scientists taught the nestlings how to survive in the wild. Then they put name bands around the legs of each bird and let them go.

One of the birds landed on a ledge of Baltimore's tallest office building. No one there knew what kind of bird she was. She was much larger and looked very different from other birds. She bowed and screeched *ghe, ghe, ghe* at her reflection in the windows. Then she sat and dozed for days with her feathers fluffed. Someone thought she was sick and asked an ornithologist for help.

The ornithologist recognized the bird as a peregrine falcon and saw the name bands she wore around each leg. He knew the scientists who had raised her at The Hawk Barn. The bird's name was Scarlett. She was not sick. It was almost spring, so she wanted to find a mate and start a family.

Most falcons live on high, rocky cliffs or city skyscrapers. They like wide-open areas near water where they can hunt. From atop their eyries—the places where most birds of prey live—they can easily spot their prey a mile away. They make their nests, or scrapes, by scratching away rocks to form hollow places for their eggs. Falcons keep the same eyrie for life— twenty years or more.

The people at Scarlett's office building placed a nest box on her favorite ledge, thirty-three stories above the city's rumble. There she slept, ate, and made a scrape. She had everything a peregrine could want—except a mate.

She searched endlessly for him. The weeks became months, and the months became years. The ornithologists tried to introduce mates to her, but each one either died or disappeared. But Scarlett didn't give up.

After five years of searching, one day Scarlett's life changed. A wild peregrine landed on her ledge! Immediately, they took off together. They flew wing to wing, chased each other, and soared and tumbled through the sky for days. He offered her food. She accepted it. Now they were bonded as mates for life. That spring, Scarlett laid a clutch of four eggs.

The news of Scarlett's eggs spread across the world.
Everyone who knew of Scarlett celebrated and hoped. These
were very special eggs: the first wild peregrine eggs laid in the
eastern United States in thirty years. Would they hatch?

The office people named Scarlett's mate Beauregard. The falcons took turns sitting on the eggs to keep them warm. After four weeks, the chicks began to pip through their shells. Soon the parents had four hungry eyases to feed.

Success at last for The Hawk Barn scientists, the office people, and especially Scarlett! Together, she and Beauregard successfully raised their brood of little falcons on the ledge.

Scarlett died soon after her fledgelings flew off on their own, but Beauregard still lives in the scrape that Scarlett built. And every spring, he and his new mate raise a new brood of eyases. They teach them to fly and hunt. Within a few weeks, they are ready to fly away to find mates and raise their own eyases, just as Scarlett once did.

The falcon researchers at The Hawk Barn have been well rewarded for their efforts. Peregrine falcons were thought to be extinct in the eastern United States in the 1970s, but today there are more than a hundred nesting pairs. Much of this success is due to Scarlett and the falcons born in her scrape on the ledge of a Baltimore office building.

Falcons to Watch For

Gyrfalcon *(Falco rusticolis)*

The gyrfalcon is the largest of all the falcons. It is two feet tall with a wingspan of four feet. Its colors range from pure white to dark gray. It lives on cliffs in Alaska and the Arctic. Gyrfalcons were once the prized possessions of kings, who used them in the ancient sport of hunting with falcons, known as falconry.

Peregrine Falcon *(Falco peregrinus)*

In falconry, peregrines were prized for their speed and spectacular 200-mile-per-hour stoops. They are slightly smaller than the gyrfalcon, and the "mustache" marks on their faces make them clearly different from other falcons. Peregrine falcons may migrate as far as 10,000 miles, farther than any other bird. Perhaps this is how they got the name peregrine, which means wanderer. Peregrine falcons live in many parts of the United States, particularly in the Rocky Mountains and on the East and West coasts.

American Kestrel *(Falco sparverius)*

The American kestrel is tiny for a falcon; it is about the size of a robin. It lives in most parts of the United States on open farmland, where there are plenty of insects, snakes, and small mammals to eat.

Merlin *(Falco columbarius)*

The merlin lives in forests and on prairies from Alaska to the Southwest. When it hunts songbirds, it imitates the way they fly, then catches them by surprise. The merlin is slightly larger than the American kestrel.

Prairie Falcon *(Falco mexicanus)*

The prairie falcon looks very much like the peregrine without its "mustache." Like the peregrine, it is a bold and swift hunter. It lives in the dry areas of the West.

It's Fun to Go Falcon-Watching

Find out what kind of falcon lives near you. If you live in a city, there may be a pair of peregrines nesting on a skyscraper that you can visit. Your local nature center or state department of natural resources can tell you.

There are also many places throughout the United States where you and your family can watch huge migrations of birds, including falcons. Some of the best places to falcon-watch are listed here. Contact them first for a brochure, and be sure to visit at the right time of year.

Hawk Mountain Sanctuary Association
Route 2, Box 191
Kempton, PA 19529
(610) 756–6961

Cape May Bird Observatory
P.O. Box 3
Cape May Point, NJ 08212
(609) 884–2736

Chincoteague National Wildlife Refuge
P.O. Box 62
Chincoteague, VA 23336
(804) 336–6122

The Golden Gate Raptor Observatory
Building 204, Fort Mason
San Francisco, CA 94123
(415) 331–0730

The Snake River Birds of Prey Area
Bureau of Land Management
3948 Development Ave.
Boise, ID 83705–5389
(208) 384–3300

For more information about falcons, you can contact:

World Center for Birds of Prey
5666 Flying Hawk Lane
Boise, ID 83709
(208) 362–3716